JAVASCRIPT FOR BEGINNERS

The Ultimate Step-By-Step Guide To Learning, Understanding, And Mastering JavaScript Programming Like A Pro

JAVASCRIPT FOR BEGINNERS: THE ULTIMATE STEP-BY-STEP GUIDE TO LEARNING, UNDERSTANDING, AND MASTERING JAVASCRIPT PROGRAMMING LIKE A PRO

First edition. November 29, 2023.

Written by Voltaire Lumiere.

TABLE OF CONTENTS

Introduction 1
Chapter 1: Introduction To Javascript 4
Chapter 2: Javascript Fundamentals 48
Chapter 3: Advanced Javascript Concepts... 65
Chapter 4: Building Real-World Applications 78
Chapter 5: Best Practices And Optimization 92
Conclusion 106

INTRODUCTION

Welcome to the exciting world of JavaScript, a language that has transformed the landscape of web development and continues to power the interactive experiences you encounter every day on the internet. In this comprehensive guide, "JavaScript For Beginners: The Ultimate Step-By-Step Guide To Learning, Understanding, And Mastering JavaScript Programming Like A Pro," we embark on a journey through the fundamentals, intricacies, and best practices of JavaScript programming.

Unveiling the Power of JavaScript:

JavaScript, often hailed as the "language of the web," has evolved far beyond its humble beginnings as a client-side scripting language. Its role has expanded to the server side with the advent of Node.js, making it an indispensable tool for full-stack development. As a dynamic and versatile language, JavaScript enables developers to build not only interactive websites but also scalable and performant applications across diverse domains.

The Need for JavaScript Proficiency:

In an era where user engagement is paramount, understanding JavaScript is not just an asset; it's a necessity. As you navigate through this guide, you'll unravel the core concepts of JavaScript, from the basics of variables and control flow to advanced topics like asynchronous programming and object-oriented design. Whether you're a budding developer eager to grasp the essentials or a seasoned coder aiming to enhance your skills, this guide caters to learners at every stage of their JavaScript journey.

What Sets This Guide Apart:

This isn't just another programming manual; it's your companion in the exploration of JavaScript's vast ecosystem. The guide is structured with a learner-centric approach, focusing on hands-on experience and real-world application. Each chapter is crafted to build a strong foundation, incrementally introducing concepts and reinforcing them through practical examples and milestone projects.

Learning Beyond Syntax:

While mastering the syntax is crucial, we go beyond the surface, delving into the philosophy of writing clean, maintainable code. Discover the art of problem-solving, understand the nuances of JavaScript's event-driven architecture, and explore best practices that distinguish proficient developers.

Navigating the Chapters:

Our journey unfolds across carefully crafted chapters, each serving as a stepping stone in your progression. From the basics of setting up your development environment to the intricacies of asynchronous programming and advanced concepts like closures and design patterns, this guide is your roadmap to JavaScript mastery.

Your Success Path:

As you progress through the chapters and complete milestone projects, envision the transformation from a JavaScript enthusiast to a proficient developer capable of building interactive web applications with confidence. Along the way, we'll discuss real-world scenarios, share industry insights, and equip you with the tools to tackle the challenges of modern web development.

Get ready to immerse yourself in the world of JavaScript—a language that empowers creativity, drives innovation, and shapes the digital experiences we encounter daily. Let's embark on this journey together, where learning is not just a destination but a continuous exploration of the ever-evolving JavaScript universe. Happy coding!

CHAPTER 1

INTRODUCTION TO JAVASCRIPT

JavaScript is a versatile programming language primarily known for its use in web development. It is a high-level, interpreted language that allows developers to create dynamic and interactive content within web browsers. JavaScript is one of the core technologies for building modern, responsive, and feature-rich websites and web applications.

Key characteristics of JavaScript include:

1. **Client-Side Scripting:** JavaScript is primarily executed on the client side, meaning it runs in the user's web browser. This enables dynamic updates to web pages without requiring a full page reload, providing a more interactive user experience.

2. **Object-Oriented:** JavaScript is an object-oriented language, allowing developers to work with objects and manipulate them to create sophisticated applications. It supports both prototype-based and class-based inheritance.

3. **Event-Driven:** JavaScript is event-driven, meaning it can respond to user actions, such as clicks, form submissions, or keyboard inputs. This makes it well-suited for creating interactive interfaces and handling user interactions.

4. **Asynchronous Programming:** JavaScript supports asynchronous programming through features like callbacks, promises, and async/await. This is crucial for handling tasks such as fetching data from servers without blocking the execution of other code.

5. **Cross-Platform Compatibility:** JavaScript is supported by all major web browsers, including Chrome, Firefox, Safari, and Edge. This ensures that web applications built with JavaScript can run on a wide range of devices and platforms.

6. **Libraries and Frameworks:** JavaScript has a rich ecosystem of libraries and frameworks that simplify and enhance the development process. Notable examples include jQuery, React, Angular, and Vue.js.

7. **Server-Side Development:** With the introduction of Node.js, JavaScript can now be used for server-side development as well. This allows developers to use the same language for both client-side and server-side scripting, creating a more unified development environment.

8. **Dynamic Typing:** JavaScript is a dynamically typed language, meaning variable types are determined at runtime. This flexibility allows for more rapid development but also requires careful attention to type-related issues.

JavaScript plays a central role in the creation of modern web applications, from enhancing user interfaces to enabling complex interactions with servers. Its versatility and widespread adoption make it a foundational language for web development. **Why Learn JavaScript?**

JavaScript stands as a cornerstone in the realm of web development, wielding unparalleled significance for developers and the digital landscape as a whole. Its omnipresence on the client-side of web applications empowers developers to create dynamic, interactive, and responsive user experiences. As a versatile scripting language, JavaScript seamlessly integrates with HTML and CSS, forming the trinity that underpins the modern web.

The evolution of the web from static, text-based pages to dynamic, feature-rich applications is intrinsically tied to JavaScript's capabilities. It enables real-time updates, interactive forms, and engaging user interfaces, transforming static websites into dynamic platforms that respond in real-time to user actions. JavaScript's ability to manipulate the Document Object Model (DOM) lies at the heart of this dynamism, allowing developers to alter page content and structure on the fly.

Moreover, JavaScript plays a pivotal role in enabling asynchronous communication through AJAX (Asynchronous JavaScript and XML). This facilitates the retrieval of data from servers without the need for a page refresh, contributing to a smoother and more seamless user experience. The asynchronous nature of JavaScript empowers developers to create responsive web applications that can handle multiple tasks simultaneously, enhancing performance and user satisfaction.

In the contemporary digital landscape, where user engagement and experience are paramount, learning JavaScript is not merely an option but a necessity. From small-scale projects to large-scale enterprise applications, JavaScript is the driving force behind the interactivity and responsiveness that users have come to expect. Its widespread adoption and compatibility with all major web browsers make it an indispensable skill for any aspiring web developer.

In conclusion, delving into JavaScript is a journey into the core of web development, unlocking the ability to craft dynamic, interactive, and cutting-edge digital experiences. Aspiring developers embarking on this journey are equipping themselves with a tool that has not only shaped the past and present of the web but will continue to define its future.

- **Versatility in Modern Applications**

JavaScript's versatility in modern applications is akin to an adaptive language that transcends traditional boundaries, making it an indispensable tool in the contemporary digital landscape. Its widespread applicability extends far beyond its foundational role in web development, permeating diverse domains and use cases.

One of JavaScript's key strengths lies in its capacity to operate across various platforms and environments. It serves as the scripting language not only for web browsers but also for server-side development through platforms like Node.js. This duality enables developers to leverage a single language for both client and server-side programming, fostering a unified and efficient development ecosystem.

Beyond the realm of traditional web development, JavaScript has found its way into mobile application development. Frameworks such as React Native and frameworks for progressive web apps enable developers to use JavaScript for building cross-platform mobile applications, streamlining the development process and maximizing code reuse.

Moreover, JavaScript has become a prominent player in the realm of desktop application development. With frameworks like Electron, developers can use JavaScript, along with HTML and CSS, to build desktop applications for major operating systems. This adaptability allows developers to create applications that seamlessly transition across web, mobile, and desktop environments.

JavaScript's versatility is not confined to conventional software development. It has also become a staple in the Internet of Things (IoT) ecosystem. With the advent of platforms like Johnny-Five and Node-RED, JavaScript facilitates the programming of connected devices and IoT applications, providing a bridge between the digital and physical worlds.

In the context of emerging technologies, JavaScript's adaptability is evident in its integration with machine learning and artificial intelligence frameworks. Libraries like TensorFlow.js enable developers to bring machine learning models directly into web applications, opening new frontiers for intelligent and interactive user experiences.

In essence, JavaScript's versatility extends its reach far beyond the browser, encompassing a spectrum of applications that define the digital experience in the 21st century. Aspiring developers who master JavaScript are not only equipped with a powerful tool for web development but also gain entry into a versatile ecosystem that spans diverse technological landscapes.

- **Career Opportunities**

Embarking on a journey to master JavaScript opens a gateway to a vast and dynamic realm of career opportunities, positioning individuals at the forefront of the ever-evolving tech industry. The demand for skilled JavaScript developers is not merely a trend but a fundamental need driven by the pervasive influence of web technologies across various sectors.

1. **Web Development Roles:**

- **Front-End Developer:** As a front-end developer, proficiency in JavaScript is paramount. This role involves creating visually appealing and interactive user interfaces, translating design concepts into functional web applications.

- **Full-Stack Developer:** Mastery of both front-end and back-end technologies, including JavaScript, is essential for full-stack developers. They are capable of handling all aspects of web development, from user interface design to server-side logic.

2. **Mobile App Development:**

- **React Native Developer:** With the rise of cross-platform mobile app development, JavaScript developers specializing in frameworks like React Native can create mobile applications for iOS and Android, maximizing code reuse.

- **Ionic Developer:** JavaScript developers can leverage the Ionic framework to build mobile applications with web technologies, catering to a broad audience on various mobile platforms.

3. **Desktop Application Development:**

- **Electron Developer:** JavaScript proficiency is crucial for developers using Electron to build cross-platform desktop applications. This framework allows for the creation of desktop apps using web technologies.

4. **Server-Side Development:**

- **Node.js Developer:** Node.js, a JavaScript runtime, enables server-side development. Node.js developers build scalable and efficient server-side applications, handling tasks such as data manipulation, server logic, and handling requests.

5. **IoT and Embedded Systems:**

- **IoT Developer:** JavaScript's versatility extends to the Internet of Things (IoT), where developers can use platforms like Johnny-Five and Node-RED to program connected devices, creating innovative IoT solutions.

6. **Machine Learning and AI:**

- **TensorFlow.js Developer:** JavaScript developers can integrate machine learning models into web applications using TensorFlow.js, contributing to the intersection of artificial intelligence and web technologies.

7. **Tech Education and Consulting:**

- **JavaScript Instructor/Consultant:** With expertise in JavaScript, individuals can contribute to the tech community by becoming instructors or consultants, sharing knowledge through courses, workshops, and consulting services.

8. **Freelancing and Entrepreneurship:**

- **Freelance Developer/Entrepreneur:** Mastering JavaScript opens doors to freelance opportunities and entrepreneurial ventures. Developers can offer their skills on platforms, create their applications, or even establish their tech startups.

In essence, the mastery of JavaScript not only equips individuals with technical skills but also positions them at the forefront of a diverse and expanding job market. The versatility of JavaScript ensures that career opportunities span a wide spectrum, offering professionals the flexibility to explore various domains within the tech industry.

- **Getting Started with JavaScript**

Embarking on your JavaScript journey begins with the essential step of setting up a conducive development environment. A well-configured environment lays the foundation for seamless coding, testing, and debugging. Here's a comprehensive guide to help you establish your JavaScript development space:

1. **Text Editor or Integrated Development Environment (IDE):**

- Choose a text editor or IDE that suits your preferences. Popular choices include Visual Studio Code, Sublime Text, Atom, or WebStorm.
- Customize your editor with themes, extensions, and settings that enhance your coding experience.

2. **Installing Node.js:**

- JavaScript on the server-side is powered by Node.js. Visit the official Node.js website (https://nodejs.org/) to download and install the latest stable version.
- Verify the installation by opening your terminal or command prompt and typing **node -v** and **npm -v** to check the Node.js and npm (Node Package Manager) versions, respectively.

3. **Version Control with Git:**

- Git is essential for tracking changes in your code and collaborating with others. Install Git from the official website (https://git-scm.com/).
- Familiarize yourself with basic Git commands such as **git init**, **git add**, **git commit**, and explore platforms like GitHub for remote repositories.

4. **Browser Developer Tools:**

- Chrome, Firefox, Safari, and Edge offer robust developer tools for debugging JavaScript in the browser. Familiarize yourself with these tools for efficient troubleshooting.
- Learn how to access the console, inspect elements, set breakpoints, and analyze network requests.

5. **HTML and CSS Basics:**

- JavaScript often interacts with HTML and CSS to manipulate the Document Object Model (DOM). Ensure a solid understanding of HTML for structuring content and CSS for styling.
- Create a simple HTML file linked to an external JavaScript file to practice the basics.

6. **Online Code Editors:**

- If you're getting started quickly or want to experiment without local setup, explore online code editors like CodePen, JSFiddle, or Repl.it.
- These platforms provide a sandbox environment where you can write HTML, CSS, and JavaScript code, and see instant results.

7. **Learning Resources:**

- Utilize online learning platforms and tutorials to grasp the fundamentals. Websites like MDN Web Docs,

W3Schools, and freeCodeCamp offer comprehensive guides for beginners.

- Invest time in understanding core JavaScript concepts such as variables, data types, control flow, and functions.

8. **Community Engagement:**

- Join JavaScript forums and communities like Stack Overflow, Reddit (r/javascript), or local meetups.
- Engage in discussions, seek help when needed, and learn from the experiences of other developers.

By meticulously setting up your development environment and familiarizing yourself with the tools at your disposal, you pave the way for a smooth and productive JavaScript learning experience. These foundational steps will empower you to dive into the world of JavaScript programming with confidence and enthusiasm.

- **Your First JavaScript Program**

Congratulations on taking the first step in your JavaScript journey! Now, let's write your very first JavaScript program. Follow these simple steps to create a basic program that will introduce you to the fundamentals of JavaScript:

1. **Create an HTML File:**

- Open your preferred text editor or IDE and create a new file with the ".html" extension. This file will serve as the container for your HTML and JavaScript code.

2. **Write HTML Structure:**

- Inside your HTML file, set up the basic structure with the following code:

```
<!DOCTYPE html>

<html lang="en">

<head>

<meta charset="UTF-8">

<meta name="viewport" content="width=device-width, initial-scale=1.0">

<title>Your First JavaScript Program</title>

</head>

<body>

<h1>Hello, JavaScript!</h1>

</body>

</html>
```

Embed JavaScript:

- To include JavaScript in your HTML file, add a **<script>** tag inside the **<body>** section, just before the closing **</body>** tag. This is where you'll write your JavaScript code.

```
<!DOCTYPE html>

<html lang="en">

<head>

<meta charset="UTF-8">

<meta name="viewport" content="width=device-width, initial-scale=1.0">

<title>Your First JavaScript Program</title>

</head>

<body>

<h1>Hello, JavaScript!</h1>

<script>

  // Your JavaScript code will go here

</script>

</body>

</html>
```

Write Your JavaScript Code:

- Within the **<script>** tags, write a simple JavaScript statement. Let's start with the classic "Hello, World!" example:

```
<!DOCTYPE html>
<html lang="en">
<head>
<meta charset="UTF-8">
<meta name="viewport" content="width=device-width, initial-scale=1.0">
<title>Your First JavaScript Program</title>
</head>
<body>
<h1>Hello, JavaScript!</h1>
<script>
  // Your JavaScript code will go here
  console.log("Hello, World!");
</script>
</body>
</html>
```

1. **View in a Browser:**

- Save your HTML file and open it in a web browser (e.g., Chrome, Firefox, or Edge).
- Right-click on the page, select "Inspect" or "Inspect Element" to open the browser's developer tools.
- Navigate to the "Console" tab, where you should see the output "Hello, World!" logged.

2. **Understanding the Code:**

- In the JavaScript code, **console.log("Hello, World!");** is a simple statement that outputs the text "Hello, World!" to the browser's console. The **console.log()** function is a valuable tool for displaying information while developing.

Congratulations! You've successfully written and executed your first JavaScript program. This simple yet powerful exercise sets the stage for exploring more complex JavaScript concepts and building interactive web applications. As you progress, continue experimenting with code and exploring the vast possibilities that JavaScript offers.

- **Understanding Basic Syntax**

As you delve into JavaScript, understanding its basic syntax is crucial for expressing logic and creating functional code. Here's a comprehensive overview of the fundamental syntax elements in JavaScript:

1. **Comments:**

- Use // for single-line comments and /* */ for multi-line comments.

```
// This is a single-line comment
/*
This is a
multi-line comment
*/
```

Variables:

- Declare variables using **var**, **let**, or **const**.
- **var** has function scope, **let** has block scope, and **const** is used for constants.

```
var x = 10;
let y = "Hello";
const PI = 3.14;
```

Data Types:

- JavaScript has dynamic typing, and variables can hold different types of values.
- Common data types include numbers, strings, booleans, objects, arrays, and null.

```
let num = 42;

let str = "JavaScript";

let bool = true;

let arr = [1, 2, 3];

let obj = { key: "value" };

let n = null;
```

Operators:

- Use operators for arithmetic, assignment, comparison, logical operations, etc.

```
let sum = 5 + 3;

let product = 10 * 2;

let isEqual = (5 === 5); // Comparison operator

let andOperator = (true && false); // Logical AND
```

Conditional Statements:

- Employ **if**, **else if**, and **else** for decision-making in your code.

```
let num = 10;

if (num > 0) {

console.log("Positive");

} else if (num < 0) {
```

```
console.log("Negative");
} else {
console.log("Zero");
}
```

Loops:

- Use **for**, **while**, or **do-while** to create loops.

```
for (let i = 0; i < 5; i++) {
console.log(i);
}
let counter = 0;
while (counter < 3) {
console.log(counter);
counter++;
}
```

Functions:

- Define functions to encapsulate and reuse code.

```
function greet(name) {
return "Hello, " + name + "!";
}
```

```
let greeting = greet("World");

console.log(greeting);
```

Arrays:

- Create and manipulate arrays to store collections of data.

```
let fruits = ["Apple", "Banana", "Orange"];

fruits.push("Mango");
```

Objects:

- Define objects using key-value pairs to structure data.

```
let person = {

name: "John",

age: 25,

isStudent: false

};
```

1. **Strings:**

- Manipulate strings using various methods and operators.

```
let greeting = "Hello";

let name = "John";

let message = greeting + ", " + name + "!";
```

11. **Scope:**

- Understand variable scope, including global and local scope.

```
let globalVar = "I'm global";
function example() {
let localVar = "I'm local";
console.log(globalVar); // Accessible
}
console.log(localVar); // Error: localVar is not defined
```

This overview provides a solid foundation for grasping JavaScript's basic syntax. As you progress, delve deeper into each concept and explore more advanced features to enhance your proficiency in the language. Practice writing code, experiment with different scenarios, and gradually build your JavaScript skills.

- **Variables and Data Types**

In JavaScript, variables are used to store and manipulate data. Before you can use a variable, you need to declare it. Here's a guide on declaring variables and understanding data types:

1. **Declaring Variables:**

- Use **var**, **let**, or **const** to declare variables.
- **var** has function scope, **let** has block scope, and **const** is used for constants.

```
var x = 5;  // Function-scoped variable
```

let y = "Hello, JavaScript!"; // Block-scoped variable

const PI = 3.14; // Constant (cannot be reassigned)

- Prefer **let** and **const** over **var** for better scoping and to avoid unexpected behavior.

2. **Naming Conventions:**

- Choose descriptive and meaningful names for variables.
- Follow camelCase or snake_case conventions.

let myNumber = 42; // camelCase

const MAX_COUNT = 100; // Uppercase with underscores (snake_case) for constants

Assigning Values:

- Assign values to variables using the assignment operator =.

let message = "Hello, World!";

Reassigning Variables:

- Use **let** if you intend to reassign the variable, and **const** for values that should not be changed.

let count = 10;

count = count + 1; // Reassigning is allowed with let

const daysInWeek = 7;

// daysInWeek = 8; // Error: Cannot reassign const variables

Data Types:

- JavaScript has dynamic typing, allowing variables to hold different types of values.

```
let numberVar = 42; // Number
let stringVar = "JavaScript"; // String
let booleanVar = true; // Boolean
let arrayVar = [1, 2, 3]; // Array
let objectVar = { key: "value" }; // Object
let nullVar = null; // Null
```

Type Coercion:

- JavaScript performs type coercion, converting values between types implicitly.

```
let result = "5" + 3; // "53" (string concatenation)
```

- Be mindful of type coercion to avoid unexpected results. Use explicit conversions when necessary.

2. **Hoisting:**

- Variable declarations using **var** are hoisted to the top of their scope.

```
console.log(a); // undefined
```

var a = 5;

- While the variable is hoisted, its assignment isn't. **let** and **const** are not hoisted in the same way, providing more predictable behavior.

Understanding how to declare variables and work with different data types is foundational for writing effective JavaScript code. As you progress, explore more advanced concepts related to variables and data manipulation to enhance your coding skills.

- **Data Types in JavaScript**

JavaScript is a dynamically-typed language, meaning variables can hold values of different types, and the type of a variable can change during runtime. Here's an overview of the primary data types in JavaScript:

1. **Number:**

- Represents numeric values, including integers and floating-point numbers.

let age = 25;

let temperature = 98.6;

String:

- Represents sequences of characters, enclosed in single or double quotes.

let name = "John";

let message = 'Hello, JavaScript!';

Boolean:

- Represents a logical value, either **true** or **false**.

let isStudent = true;

let hasLicense = false;

Null:

- Represents the absence of a value or a null object reference.

let emptyValue = null;

Undefined:

- Represents a variable that has been declared but not assigned a value.

let undefinedVar;

Object:

- Represents a collection of key-value pairs. Objects are used to group related data and functions.

let person = {

name: "Alice",

age: 30,

isStudent: false

};

Array:

- Represents an ordered list of values.

```
let numbers = [1, 2, 3, 4, 5];
let fruits = ["apple", "banana", "orange"];
```

Function:

- Represents a reusable block of code. Functions are a fundamental building block of JavaScript.

```
function addNumbers(a, b) {
return a + b;
}
```

Symbol:

- Introduced in ECMAScript 6, symbols represent a unique identifier.

```
const mySymbol = Symbol("description");
```

BigInt:

- Also introduced in ECMAScript 6, BigInt is used to represent integers of arbitrary precision.

```
const bigNumber = BigInt(Number.MAX_SAFE_INTEGER) + 1n;
```

Understanding data types is essential for effective JavaScript programming. JavaScript's dynamic typing allows for flexibility but requires careful consideration to avoid unexpected behavior. As you work with variables and manipulate data, be mindful of type conversions and choose the appropriate data type for the task at hand.

- **Type Coercion and Conversion**

Type coercion and conversion in JavaScript are fundamental concepts that involve changing the type of a value from one data type to another. Understanding how JavaScript handles these operations is crucial for avoiding unexpected behavior in your code.

1. **Type Coercion:**

- Type coercion in JavaScript refers to the automatic conversion of values from one data type to another during runtime. This occurs in situations where operators or functions expect a certain type of data.

let result = "5" + 3; // "53" (string concatenation)

- In the example above, the addition operator is used with a string and a number. JavaScript automatically converts the number to a string and performs string concatenation.

2. **Explicit Conversion:**

- You can perform explicit type conversion using functions like **Number()**, **String()**, or **Boolean()** to convert values to a specific type.

let numString = "10";

let num = Number(numString); // Explicit conversion to a number

let boolValue = Boolean("Hello"); // Explicit conversion to a Boolean

Implicit Conversion:

- Some operations in JavaScript implicitly perform type coercion. For example, using the == operator may perform type coercion if the operands have different types.

console.log(5 == "5"); // true (implicit coercion)

- In the example above, JavaScript performs type coercion to compare the values, resulting in a **true** comparison.

2. **Truthy and Falsy Values:**

- JavaScript has truthy and falsy values. Falsy values are implicitly converted to **false** in a boolean context, while truthy values are converted to **true**.

if (0) {

// This block will not be executed because 0 is a falsy value

```
}
if ("Hello") {
// This block will be executed because "Hello" is a truthy value
}
```

String Conversion:

- When a non-string value is used in a string context (e.g., with the + operator for string concatenation), JavaScript implicitly converts the value to a string.

```
let age = 25;
let message = "I am " + age + " years old."; // Implicit string conversion
```

Numeric Conversion:

- When a non-numeric value is used in a numeric context, JavaScript implicitly converts the value to a number.

```
let numericString = "42";
let sum = 10 + numericString; // Implicit numeric conversion
```

Understanding type coercion and conversion is crucial for writing robust and predictable JavaScript code. While JavaScript's flexibility allows for dynamic typing, developers should be aware of the potential pitfalls and use explicit conversion when needed to ensure code clarity and correctness.

- **Control Flow and Loops**
- **Conditional Statements**

Conditional statements in JavaScript allow you to control the flow of your program based on certain conditions. They enable you to make decisions and execute different blocks of code depending on whether a specified condition evaluates to true or false. Here are the primary conditional statements in JavaScript:

1. **If Statement:**

- The **if** statement is the most basic form of a conditional statement. It executes a block of code if the specified condition is true.

For example: "If it's sunny, go for a walk."

2. **If-Else Statement:**

- The **if-else** statement allows you to specify two blocks of code: one to be executed if the condition is true, and another if the condition is false.

For example: "If it's raining, take an umbrella; otherwise, leave it at home."

3. **If-Else If-Else Statement:**

- Use the **if-else if-else** statement when you have multiple conditions to check. It provides a sequence of conditions, and the first true condition's block is executed.

For example: "If the time is before noon, say 'Good morning'; else if it's before 6 PM, say 'Good afternoon'; otherwise, say 'Good evening'."

4. **Switch Statement:**

- The **switch** statement is useful when you have multiple possible conditions and want to execute different blocks of code based on the value of an expression.

For example: "Switch on the day of the week: If it's Monday, say 'It's the start of the week'; if it's Friday, say 'TGIF'; otherwise, say 'It's a regular day'."

5. **Ternary Operator:**

- The ternary operator (**? :**) provides a concise way to write simple conditional statements. It's a shorthand for the **if-else** statement.

For example: "Check if the age is 18 or older. If true, say 'You are an adult'; otherwise, say 'You are a minor'."

Conditional statements are essential for building logic and making decisions in your JavaScript programs. They allow you to create dynamic, responsive code that adapts to different scenarios. As you advance, combine these statements with loops and other control flow structures for more complex program behavior.

- **Looping Structures**

Looping structures in JavaScript provide a way to execute a block of code repeatedly, enabling automation of repetitive tasks and iteration over data structures. Here are the primary looping structures in JavaScript:

1. **For Loop:** The **for** loop is used when the number of iterations is known beforehand. It consists of three parts: initialization, condition, and increment/decrement. This loop is suitable when you have a fixed number of iterations.

2. **While Loop:** The **while** loop repeats a block of code as long as a specified condition is true. It is helpful when the number of iterations is not known in advance and depends on a condition.

3. **Do-While Loop:** Similar to the **while** loop, the **do-while** loop always executes the block of code at least once before checking the condition. This can be useful when you want to ensure the code runs at least once.

4. **For-In Loop:** The **for-in** loop is used for iterating over the properties of an object. It enumerates the properties of an object, including inherited ones, making it useful for working with objects.

5. **For-Of Loop:** Introduced in ECMAScript 6, the **for-of** loop is used for iterating over iterable objects, such as arrays. It provides a concise syntax for iterating over the values of an iterable.

6. **Break Statement:** The **break** statement is used to exit a loop prematurely, regardless of whether the loop condition is true. It allows you to terminate the loop before completing all iterations.

7. **Continue Statement:** The **continue** statement is used to skip the rest of the code inside a loop for the current iteration and move to the next iteration. It allows you to skip specific iterations based on a condition.

Looping structures are fundamental for automating tasks and processing data in a repetitive manner. Each type of loop has its use cases, so choose the one that fits the requirements of your specific scenario.

- **Writing Efficient Code with Control Flow**

Efficient code not only produces the desired results but also minimizes resource usage and execution time. When working with control flow structures in JavaScript, consider the following tips to enhance the efficiency of your code:

1. **Use the Right Loop for the Task:**

- Choose the loop that best fits your specific use case. For example, use a **for** loop when the number of iterations is known, a **while** loop when the condition is dynamic, and a **for-of** loop when iterating over values in an array.

2. **Optimize Loop Conditions:**

- Ensure that loop conditions are efficient and do not involve unnecessary computations. Avoid complex expressions in loop conditions to improve readability and performance.

// Less efficient for (let i = 0; i < array.length * 2; i++) { // ... } // More efficient const arrayLength = array.length; for (let i = 0; i < arrayLength; i++) { // ... }

3. **Minimize Code Inside Loops:**

- Keep the code inside loops to a minimum. If possible, move variable declarations and computations outside the loop to avoid redundant assignments.

// Less efficient for (let i = 0; i < array.length; i++) { let result = array[i] * 2; // ... } // More efficient let result; for (let i = 0; i < array.length; i++) { result = array[i] * 2; // ... }

4. **Consider Early Exit:**

- Use the **break** statement when a condition is met to exit a loop early. This can be especially useful in scenarios where further iterations are unnecessary.

for (let i = 0; i < array.length; i++) { if (array[i] === targetValue) { console.log("Value found!"); break; } }

5. **Switch for Multiple Conditions:**

- When dealing with multiple conditions, consider using a **switch** statement instead of a series of **if-else if** statements. This can lead to more efficient and readable code.

```
switch (dayOfWeek) { case "Monday": // ... break; case "Tuesday": // ... break; // ... default: // ... }
```

6. **Use Ternary Operators Wisely:**

- Ternary operators can make code concise, but using them excessively can reduce readability. Use ternary operators for simple conditions and consider traditional **if-else** statements for more complex logic.

```
// Less efficient let result = (x > 0) ? "Positive" : "Non-positive"; // More efficient let result; if (x > 0) { result = "Positive"; } else { result = "Non-positive"; }
```

7. **Profile and Optimize:**

- Use browser developer tools to profile your code and identify performance bottlenecks. Optimize the critical sections of your code to improve overall efficiency.

```
// Profile your code using browser developer tools console.time("Loop Execution"); for (let i = 0; i < 1000000; i++) { // Code to be profiled } console.timeEnd("Loop Execution");
```

Applying these tips will help you write control flow structures that not only produce correct results but also contribute to the overall efficiency of your JavaScript code. Always balance readability and maintainability with performance considerations.

- **Functions in JavaScript**

Functions in JavaScript are reusable blocks of code that perform a specific task or return a value. They play a crucial role in organizing and structuring code. Here's a guide on declaring and invoking functions in JavaScript:

1. **Declaring a Function:**

- You can declare a function using the **function** keyword, followed by the function name, parameters (if any), and the function body.

```
function greet(name) { console.log("Hello, " + name + "!");
}
```

In this example, **greet** is the function name, and it takes a parameter **name**.

2. **Invoking (Calling) a Function:**

- After declaring a function, you can invoke or call it to execute the code inside the function body.

```
greet("John");
```

This invocation of the **greet** function with the argument "John" will print "Hello, John!" to the console.

3. **Function with Return Value:**

- Functions can also return a value using the **return** keyword. The returned value can be stored in a variable or used in further computations.

function add(x, y) { return x + y; } let sum = add(3, 5); console.log(sum); // Output: 8

The **add** function takes two parameters and returns their sum.

4. **Function Expressions:**

- Functions can be assigned to variables, creating what's known as a function expression.

let multiply = function(x, y) { return x * y; }; let result = multiply(4, 6); console.log(result); // Output: 24

In this example, **multiply** is a variable holding a function.

5. **Arrow Functions (ES6+):**

- Arrow functions provide a more concise syntax for writing functions, especially for simple one-liners.

let square = (num) => num * num; let squaredValue = square(5); console.log(squaredValue); // Output: 25

Arrow functions are particularly useful for short, anonymous functions.

6. **Default Parameters (ES6+):**

- You can provide default values for function parameters, which will be used if the corresponding argument is not passed during the function call.

function greet(name = "Guest") { console.log("Hello, " + name + "!"); } greet(); // Output: Hello, Guest! greet("John"); // Output: Hello, John!

The **name** parameter has a default value of "Guest."

7. **Rest Parameters (ES6+):**

- The rest parameter allows a function to accept an indefinite number of arguments as an array.

function sumNumbers(...numbers) { return numbers.reduce((total, num) => total + num, 0); } let totalSum = sumNumbers(1, 2, 3, 4, 5); console.log(totalSum); // Output: 15

The **...numbers** syntax gathers the provided arguments into an array.

Functions are fundamental building blocks in JavaScript, providing a way to encapsulate and reuse code. They contribute to code modularity, readability, and maintainability. Experiment with different types of functions to understand their versatility and use them effectively in your projects.

- **Parameters and Return Statements**

Parameters and return statements enhance the functionality of JavaScript functions, allowing them to accept input values and produce output. Here's a detailed exploration of parameters and return statements in functions:

1. **Function Parameters:**

- Parameters are placeholders for values that a function expects to receive when it is called. They are listed in the function declaration and act as variables within the function scope.

```
function greet(name) { console.log("Hello, " + name + "!"); }
```

In this example, **name** is a parameter that the **greet** function expects.

2. **Default Parameters (ES6+):**

- Default parameters allow you to assign default values to parameters, which are used when the corresponding argument is not provided during the function call.

```
function greet(name = "Guest") { console.log("Hello, " + name + "!"); }
```

If no **name** is provided, the default value "Guest" is used.

3. **Function Arguments:**

- Arguments are the actual values passed to a function when it is invoked. They correspond to the parameters in the function declaration.

greet("John");

Here, "John" is the argument passed to the **greet** function.

4. **Multiple Parameters:**

- Functions can have multiple parameters separated by commas.

function add(x, y) { console.log(x + y); } add(3, 5); // Output: 8

The **add** function takes two parameters, **x** and **y**.

5. **Return Statements:**

- The **return** statement allows a function to send a value back to the code that called it. It also terminates the function's execution.

function square(x) { return x * x; } let result = square(4); console.log(result); // Output: 16

The **square** function returns the square of the input **x**.

6. **Returning Multiple Values:**

- While a function can only have one return value, you can return an object or an array to effectively return multiple values.

function calculateStats(numbers) { let sum = numbers.reduce((total, num) => total + num, 0); let average = sum / numbers.length; return { sum, average }; } let stats = calculateStats([2, 4, 6, 8, 10]); console.log(stats.sum); // Output: 30 console.log(stats.average); // Output: 6

The **calculateStats** function returns an object containing the sum and average.

7. **Return Statement Without a Value:**

- A function can have a **return** statement without a value. In this case, it will return **undefined**.

function noReturnValue() { console.log("This function does not return a value."); // No return statement with a value } let result = noReturnValue(); console.log(result); // Output: undefined

The **noReturnValue** function does not explicitly return a value.

Understanding how parameters and return statements work in JavaScript functions is essential for creating flexible and reusable code. Utilize them to make your functions more versatile and capable of handling a variety of scenarios.

- **Scope and Function Expressions**

Understanding scope and function expressions is crucial for writing maintainable and modular JavaScript code. Let's delve into these concepts:

1. **Scope in JavaScript:**

- Scope refers to the context in which variables are declared and accessed. JavaScript has two main types of scope: global scope and local (function) scope.

// Global Scope let globalVar = "I'm global!"; function exampleFunction() { // Local Scope let localVar = "I'm local!"; console.log(globalVar); // Accessible } console.log(globalVar); // Accessible console.log(localVar); // Error: localVar is not defined

Variables declared outside of any function or block have global scope, while those declared within a function have local scope.

2. **Function Expressions:**

- Function expressions involve defining a function as part of an expression. They can be anonymous or have a name.

// Anonymous Function Expression let greet = function(name) { console.log("Hello, " + name + "!"); }; // Named Function Expression let add = function sum(a, b) { return a + b; };

In the first example, **greet** is an anonymous function expression, and in the second example, **add** is a named function expression.

Function expressions are useful for creating functions dynamically or passing them as arguments.

3. **Function Scope:**

- Variables declared within a function using **var** have function scope. This means they are accessible only within that function.

function exampleFunction() { var functionVar = "I'm function-scoped!"; console.log(functionVar); // Accessible } console.log(functionVar); // Error: functionVar is not defined

The use of **let** and **const** introduced block scope, making variables accessible only within the block in which they are defined.

4. **Lexical Scope (Closures):**

- Lexical scope refers to the ability of a function to access variables from its outer (enclosing) scope even after the outer function has finished executing.

function outerFunction() { let outerVar = "I'm from outer!"; function innerFunction() { console.log(outerVar); // Accessing outerVar from lexical scope } return innerFunction; } let closureExample = outerFunction(); closureExample(); // Output: I'm from outer!

In this example, **innerFunction** forms a closure, allowing it to access the **outerVar** even after **outerFunction** has completed execution.

5. **Immediately Invoked Function Expressions (IIFE):**

- An IIFE is a function expression that is immediately executed after being defined. It is often used to create a private scope for variables.

(function() { let privateVar = "I'm private!"; console.log(privateVar); // Accessible within the IIFE })(); console.log(privateVar); // Error: privateVar is not defined

The variables declared within the IIFE are not accessible outside of it, providing a way to encapsulate functionality.

Understanding scope and function expressions is vital for writing robust and maintainable JavaScript code. Properly managing scope helps avoid variable conflicts and unintended side effects, while function expressions offer flexibility and allow for the creation of modular and reusable code.

CHAPTER 2

JAVASCRIPT FUNDAMENTALS

- **Objects and Arrays**

Creating and Manipulating Objects:

1. **Object Creation:**

- Objects in JavaScript are key-value pairs, allowing you to group related data and functionality.

```
let person = { name: "John", age: 30, isStudent: false };
```

This **person** object has properties like **name**, **age**, and **isStudent**.

2. **Accessing Object Properties:**

- Access object properties using dot notation or bracket notation.

```
console.log(person.name); // Dot notation console.log(person["age"]); // Bracket notation
```

3. **Adding and Modifying Properties:**

- You can add new properties or modify existing ones.

```
person.job = "Developer"; // Adding a new property person.age = 31; // Modifying an existing property
```

4. **Deleting Properties:**

- Use the **delete** keyword to remove a property from an object.

```
delete person.isStudent;
```

Working with Arrays:

1. **Array Creation:**

- Arrays are ordered lists of values.

```
let colors = ["red", "green", "blue"];
```

This **colors** array contains strings.

2. **Accessing Array Elements:**

- Access elements by their index, starting from 0.

```
console.log(colors[0]); // Output: "red"
```

3. **Adding and Removing Elements:**

- Use **push** to add elements to the end and **pop** to remove the last element.

```
colors.push("yellow"); // Add "yellow" to the end let removedColor = colors.pop(); // Remove and get the last element
```

4. **Iterating Through Arrays:**

- Use loops or array methods like **forEach** to iterate through array elements.

```
for (let i = 0; i < colors.length; i++) { console.log(colors[i]); } colors.forEach(color => console.log(color));
```

Iterating Through Objects and Arrays:

1. **Iterating Through Object Properties:**

- Use **for...in** loop to iterate through object properties.

```
for (let key in person) { console.log(key, person[key]); }
```

2. **Iterating Through Array Elements:**

- Use **for...of** loop to iterate through array elements.

```
for (let color of colors) { console.log(color); }
```

3. **Array Methods for Iteration:**

- Array methods like **forEach**, **map**, and **filter** simplify iteration.

```
colors.forEach(color => console.log(color)); let doubledNumbers = numbers.map(number => number * 2); let filteredNumbers = numbers.filter(number => number > 5);
```

4. **Object and Array Destructuring (ES6+):**

- Destructuring allows you to extract values from objects and arrays easily.

```
// Object Destructuring let { name, age } = person; // Array Destructuring let [firstColor, secondColor] = colors;
```

Objects and arrays are fundamental data structures in JavaScript. Mastering their creation, manipulation, and iteration will empower you to work effectively with complex data in your applications.

- **Understanding the Document Object Model (DOM)**

Understanding the Document Object Model (DOM):

1. **Introduction to the DOM:**

- The Document Object Model (DOM) is a programming interface that represents the structure of an HTML or XML document as a tree of objects. It provides a way for scripts to interact with the content of a web page.

2. **DOM Tree Structure:**

- The DOM tree consists of nodes representing various parts of the document, such as elements, attributes, and text. Elements are organized in a hierarchical structure.

<!-- Example HTML structure --> <html> <head> <title>Document</title> </head> <body> <h1>Hello, World!</h1> </body> </html>

In this example, the DOM tree would have nodes for **html**, **head**, **title**, **body**, and **h1**.

Selecting and Manipulating DOM Elements:

1. **Selecting Elements:**

- JavaScript allows you to select DOM elements using various methods like **getElementById**, **getElementsByClassName**, **getElementsByTagName**, **querySelector**, and **querySelectorAll**.

let headerElement = document.getElementById("header"); let allParagraphs = document.getElementsByTagName("p"); let firstDiv = document.querySelector("div");

2. **Manipulating Elements:**

- You can manipulate DOM elements by changing their properties, attributes, or content.

headerElement.innerText = "New Heading"; firstDiv.classList.add("highlight");

3. **Creating and Appending Elements:**

- Use **createElement** to create new elements and **appendChild** to add them to the DOM.

let newParagraph = document.createElement("p"); newParagraph.innerText = "This is a new paragraph."; document.body.appendChild(newParagraph);

Handling Events with JavaScript:

1. **Event Handling Basics:**

- JavaScript allows you to respond to user actions (events) on a web page. Common events include clicks, mouse movements, and keyboard input.

```
let button = document.getElementById("myButton"); button.addEventListener("click", function() { alert("Button Clicked!"); });
```

2. **Event Object:**

- When an event occurs, an event object is created. This object contains information about the event, such as the target element and the type of the event.

```
document.addEventListener("keydown", function(event) { console.log("Key pressed: " + event.key); });
```

3. **Event Propagation:**

- Events in the DOM propagate through phases: capturing, target, and bubbling. Understanding these phases is essential for effective event handling.

```
document.addEventListener("click", function() { console.log("Document Clicked!"); }, true); // Use capturing phase button.addEventListener("click", function(event) {
```

event.stopPropagation(); // Stop event from further propagation console.log("Button Clicked!"); });

4. **Removing Event Listeners:**

- It's important to remove event listeners when they are no longer needed to avoid memory leaks.

function handleClick() { alert("Button Clicked!"); } button.addEventListener("click", handleClick); // Remove the event listener button.removeEventListener("click", handleClick);

Understanding the DOM and handling events is fundamental to creating interactive and dynamic web pages with JavaScript. These concepts empower developers to manipulate page content, respond to user actions, and create a more engaging user experience.

- **Error Handling and Debugging**

1. **Syntax Errors:**

- Occur when there is a mistake in the structure of the code, such as missing parentheses or a typo.

let x = 5; console.log(x; // SyntaxError: missing) after argument list

2. **Reference Errors:**

- Happen when trying to access a variable or function that is not defined.

console.log(y); // ReferenceError: y is not defined

3. **Type Errors:**

- Arise when attempting an operation on a value of the wrong type.

let x = "Hello"; x.toUpperCase(); // TypeError: x.toUpperCase is not a function

4. **Range Errors:**

- Occur when trying to manipulate an object with a length outside its valid range.

let array = [1, 2, 3]; array[5] = 6; // RangeError: Invalid array length

Debugging Techniques:

1. **Using console.log:**

- Print values and messages to the console to understand the flow and state of the program.

let x = 10; console.log("Value of x:", x);

2. **Setting Breakpoints:**

- Use browser developer tools to set breakpoints in your code, allowing you to pause execution and inspect variables.

function multiply(a, b) { debugger; // Pause execution here return a * b; }

3. **Step Through Code:**

- Use debugger tools to step through code line by line, observing variable values and execution flow.

4. **Try-Catch Blocks for Error Handling:**

- Wrap potentially error-prone code in a try-catch block to handle errors gracefully.

```
try { // Code that may throw an error } catch (error) { // Handle the error console.error(error.message); }
```

Best Practices for Error Handling:

1. **Provide Descriptive Error Messages:**

- Clearly communicate the nature of the error to aid debugging.

```
function divide(x, y) { if (y === 0) { throw new Error("Cannot divide by zero"); } return x / y; }
```

2. **Use Meaningful Variable and Function Names:**

- Naming conventions that reflect the purpose of variables and functions enhance code readability and reduce the likelihood of errors.

```
function calculateArea(radius) { return Math.PI * radius ** 2; }
```

3. **Validate Inputs:**

- Check input values for validity before performing operations on them.

```
function fetchData(url) { if (typeof url !== "string" || !url.startsWith("http")) { throw new TypeError("Invalid URL"); } // Fetch data... }
```

4. **Log Errors Consistently:**

- Use consistent error logging to simplify debugging and monitoring.

```
try { // Code that may throw an error } catch (error) { console.error("Error caught:", error); }
```

5. **Test Thoroughly:**

- Implement unit tests and conduct thorough testing to identify and address potential issues before deploying code.

```
// Test case for the divide function it("should handle division by zero", () => { expect(() => divide(10, 0)).to.throw("Cannot divide by zero"); });
```

Effective error handling and debugging are essential for maintaining code reliability and identifying issues during development. By adopting these best practices and utilizing debugging tools, developers can streamline the debugging process and create more robust and resilient JavaScript code.

- **Asynchronous JavaScript**

1. **Callbacks:**

- Callbacks are functions passed as arguments to other functions and executed after the completion of a task.

function fetchData(callback) { // Simulating asynchronous operation setTimeout(() => { const data = "Async data"; callback(data); }, 1000); } fetchData((result) => { console.log(result); });

2. **Promises:**

- Promises provide a more structured way to handle asynchronous operations. They can be in one of three states: pending, fulfilled, or rejected.

function fetchData() { return new Promise((resolve, reject) => { // Simulating asynchronous operation setTimeout(() => { const success = true; if (success) { resolve("Async data"); } else { reject("Error fetching data"); } }, 1000); }); } fetchData() .then((result) => { console.log(result); }) .catch((error) => { console.error(error); });

Async/Await Syntax:

1. **Async Function:**

- The **async** keyword is used to define asynchronous functions. These functions always return a promise.

async function fetchData() { return "Async data"; }

2. **Await Expression:**

- The **await** keyword is used inside an async function to wait for the resolution of a promise. It can only be used within async functions.

async function fetchData() { // Simulating asynchronous operation const data = await new Promise((resolve) => { setTimeout(() => { resolve("Async data"); }, 1000); }); console.log(data); } fetchData();

Handling Asynchronous Operations:

1. **Chaining Promises:**

- Chain multiple asynchronous operations using **.then()** to create a sequence of tasks.

fetchData() .then((result) => { console.log(result); return anotherAsyncOperation(); }) .then((result) => { console.log(result); }) .catch((error) => { console.error(error); });

2. **Parallel Execution:**

- Use **Promise.all()** to run multiple asynchronous operations in parallel.

Promise.all([asyncOperation1(), asyncOperation2()]) .then((results) => { console.log(results[0], results[1]); }) .catch((error) => { console.error(error); });

3. **Async/Await for Conciseness:**

- Async/await syntax simplifies the handling of asynchronous operations, making code more readable and concise.

async function fetchData() { try { const result = await new Promise((resolve) => { setTimeout(() => { resolve("Async data"); }, 1000); }); console.log(result); } catch (error) { console.error(error); } } fetchData();

4. **Error Handling with Async/Await:**

- Use try-catch blocks for error handling in async functions.

async function fetchData() { try { const result = await new Promise((resolve, reject) => { // Simulating an error setTimeout(() => { reject("Error fetching data"); }, 1000); }); console.log(result); } catch (error) { console.error(error); } } fetchData();

Asynchronous JavaScript is crucial for handling time-consuming operations without blocking the execution of other tasks. Callbacks, promises, and async/await syntax provide different approaches to managing asynchronous code, allowing developers to choose the method that best suits their coding style and the complexity of their applications.

- **Introduction to AJAX**

1. **What is AJAX?**

- AJAX (Asynchronous JavaScript and XML) is a set of technologies that enables web pages to make asynchronous requests to a server and update parts of the page without requiring a full page reload.

2. **Why Use AJAX?**

- AJAX allows for a smoother and more dynamic user experience by fetching and displaying data in the background without interrupting the user's interaction with the page.

Making Asynchronous Requests:

1. **Using XMLHttpRequest (XHR):**

- The XMLHttpRequest object is the traditional way to make asynchronous requests in JavaScript.

let xhr = new XMLHttpRequest(); xhr.open("GET", "https://api.example.com/data", true); xhr.onreadystatechange = function () { if (xhr.readyState === 4 && xhr.status === 200) { console.log(xhr.responseText); } }; xhr.send();

2. **Fetch API (Modern Approach):**

- The Fetch API is a more modern and flexible way to make asynchronous requests.

```
fetch("https://api.example.com/data") .then((response) => { if (!response.ok) { throw new Error("Network response was not ok"); } return response.json(); }) .then((data) => { console.log(data); }) .catch((error) => { console.error("Fetch error:", error); });
```

Handling Responses:

1. **JSON Parsing:**

- When working with JSON data, parse the response to JavaScript objects.

```
fetch("https://api.example.com/data") .then((response) => response.json()) .then((data) => { console.log(data); }) .catch((error) => { console.error("Fetch error:", error); });
```

2. **Handling XML Responses (XHR):**

- If the server returns XML, use the DOMParser to parse the XML response.

```
let xhr = new XMLHttpRequest(); xhr.open("GET", "https://api.example.com/data.xml", true); xhr.onreadystatechange = function () { if (xhr.readyState === 4 && xhr.status === 200) { let xmlDoc = new DOMParser().parseFromString(xhr.responseText, "text/xml"); console.log(xmlDoc); } }; xhr.send();
```

Enhancing User Experience with AJAX:

1. **Updating Page Content Dynamically:**

- Use AJAX to update specific parts of a web page without reloading the entire page.

// Assume there is an HTML element with id="content" let contentElement = document.getElementById("content"); fetch("https://api.example.com/content") .then((response) => response.text()) .then((content) => { contentElement.innerHTML = content; }) .catch((error) => { console.error("Fetch error:", error); });

2. **Loading Data on User Interaction:**

- Trigger AJAX requests based on user interactions, such as button clicks or form submissions.

// Assume there is a button with id="loadDataBtn" let loadDataBtn = document.getElementById("loadDataBtn"); loadDataBtn.addEventListener("click", function () { fetch("https://api.example.com/data") .then((response) => response.json()) .then((data) => { console.log(data); }) .catch((error) => { console.error("Fetch error:", error); }); });

3. **Asynchronous Form Submission:**

- Prevent the default form submission and use AJAX to submit form data asynchronously.

// Assume there is a form with id="myForm" let myForm = document.getElementById("myForm");

```
myForm.addEventListener("submit", function (event) { event.preventDefault(); fetch("https://api.example.com/submit", { method: "POST", body: new FormData(myForm), }) .then((response) => response.json()) .then((result) => { console.log(result); }) .catch((error) => { console.error("Fetch error:", error); }); });
```

AJAX plays a crucial role in creating modern and dynamic web applications. It enables developers to fetch data, update page content, and enhance user interactions seamlessly. By understanding the basics of AJAX, making asynchronous requests, handling responses, and applying these techniques to improve the user experience, developers can create more responsive and interactive web applications.

CHAPTER 3

ADVANCED JAVASCRIPT CONCEPTS

- **Closures and Lexical Scoping**

1. **Definition of Closures:**

- A closure is a function bundled together with references to its surrounding state (lexical environment). It allows a function to access variables from an outer function, even after that outer function has finished execution.

function outerFunction() { let outerVariable = "I'm from the outer function"; function innerFunction() { console.log(outerVariable); } return innerFunction; } let closureExample = outerFunction(); closureExample(); // Output: I'm from the outer function

2. **Closure in Action:**

- In the example, **innerFunction** forms a closure, capturing and retaining a reference to the **outerVariable** even after **outerFunction** has completed execution. When **closureExample** is invoked, it still has access to **outerVariable**.

Lexical Scoping in JavaScript:

1. **Definition of Lexical Scoping:**

- Lexical scoping is a way to resolve variable names by looking at the nesting structure of functions in the code. In JavaScript, functions are executed using the scope they were defined in, not the scope they are called in.

function outerFunction() { let outerVariable = "I'm from the outer function"; function innerFunction() { console.log(outerVariable); } innerFunction(); } outerFunction(); // Output: I'm from the outer function

2. **Lexical Scope Example:**

- In the example, **innerFunction** has access to the variables in its lexical scope, which includes the **outerVariable** defined in the outer function.

Practical Examples:

1. **Creating Private Variables:**

- Closures are often used to create private variables that are not directly accessible from the outside.

function counter() { let count = 0; return function () { count++; console.log(count); }; } let increment = counter(); increment(); // Output: 1 increment(); // Output: 2

2. **Event Handling:**

- Closures are frequently employed in event handling to maintain state information.

function clickHandler() { let count = 0; return function () { count++; console.log(`Button clicked ${count} times`); }; } let buttonClick = clickHandler(); document.getElementById("myButton").addEventListener("click", buttonClick);

3. **Functional Programming:**

- Closures are integral to functional programming concepts like currying and partial application.

function add(x) { return function (y) { return x + y; }; } let addFive = add(5); console.log(addFive(3)); // Output: 8

Closures and lexical scoping are powerful concepts in JavaScript, enabling the creation of modular and encapsulated code. They are essential for understanding how variables are accessed and maintained in different execution contexts. By leveraging closures, developers can design more flexible and maintainable code structures.

- **ES6 and Beyond**

1. **Arrow Function Syntax:**

- Arrow functions provide a concise syntax for writing functions.

// Traditional function function add(x, y) { return x + y; } // Arrow function const add = (x, y) => x + y;

2. **No Binding of this:**

- Arrow functions do not bind their own **this** value, making them suitable for use in certain contexts, such as callbacks.

function Person() { this.age = 0; setInterval(() => { this.age++; // 'this' refers to the Person instance }, 1000); } let person = new Person();

Template Literals:

1. **String Interpolation:**

- Template literals allow embedding expressions inside string literals.

let name = "John"; let greeting = `Hello, ${name}!`; console.log(greeting); // Output: Hello, John!

2. **Multiline Strings:**

- Template literals support multiline strings without the need for concatenation.

let multilineString = ` This is a multiline string using template literals. `;

Destructuring Assignment and Spread/Rest Operators:

1. **Destructuring Assignment:**

- Destructuring allows extracting values from arrays or properties from objects in a more concise manner.

// Array destructuring let numbers = [1, 2, 3]; let [a, b, c] = numbers; // Object destructuring let person = { name: "Alice", age: 30 }; let { name, age } = person;

2. **Spread Operator:**

- The spread operator (**...**) is used to spread elements of an iterable (like an array) or properties of an object.

// Spread in arrays let arr1 = [1, 2, 3]; let arr2 = [...arr1, 4, 5]; // Spread in objects let obj1 = { a: 1, b: 2 }; let obj2 = { ...obj1, c: 3 };

3. **Rest Operator:**

- The rest operator (**...**) is used to collect remaining elements into a single array or gather remaining properties into a single object.

// Rest in function parameters (collects remaining arguments into an array) function sum(...numbers) { return numbers.reduce((total, num) => total + num, 0); } // Rest in object destructuring (gathers remaining properties into 'rest') let { a, b, ...rest } = { a: 1, b: 2, c: 3, d: 4 };

These ES6 features, including arrow functions, template literals, destructuring assignment, and spread/rest operators, enhance the readability and expressiveness of JavaScript code. Embracing these modern syntax and features contributes to more concise, maintainable, and efficient code.

- **Object-Oriented Programming (OOP) in JavaScript**

1. **Constructor Functions:**

- Constructor functions are used to create objects. They are invoked with the **new** keyword.

function Person(name, age) { this.name = name; this.age = age; } let person1 = new Person("John", 30); let person2 = new Person("Alice", 25);

2. **Prototypes:**

- Prototypes are a mechanism for object inheritance and property/method sharing.

// Adding a method to the Person prototype Person.prototype.greet = function () { console.log(`Hello, my name is ${this.name}.`); }; person1.greet(); // Output: Hello, my name is John.

Object Inheritance:

1. **Inheriting Properties and Methods:**

- Child objects can inherit properties and methods from a parent object using prototypes.

function Student(name, age, grade) { // Call the parent constructor Person.call(this, name, age); this.grade = grade; } // Inherit methods from the Person prototype Student.prototype = Object.create(Person.prototype); let student = new Student("Bob", 22, "A"); student.greet(); // Output: Hello, my name is Bob.

2. **Overriding Methods:**

- Child objects can override methods inherited from the parent.

Student.prototype.greet = function () { console.log(`Hello, I'm a student named ${this.name}.`); }; student.greet(); // Output: Hello, I'm a student named Bob.

ES6 Classes:

1. **Class Syntax:**

- ES6 introduced a more convenient syntax for constructor functions and prototypes.

class Person { constructor(name, age) { this.name = name; this.age = age; } greet() { console.log(`Hello, my name is

${this.name}.`); } } let person = new Person("Alice", 28); person.greet(); // Output: Hello, my name is Alice.

2. **Inheritance with ES6 Classes:**

- ES6 classes support a cleaner syntax for inheritance.

class Student extends Person { constructor(name, age, grade) { super(name, age); // Call the parent constructor this.grade = grade; } // Overriding the greet method greet() { console.log(`Hello, I'm a student named ${this.name}.`); } } let student = new Student("Charlie", 20, "B"); student.greet(); // Output: Hello, I'm a student named Charlie.

3. **Static Methods:**

- ES6 classes support static methods, which are called on the class itself rather than on instances.

class MathUtils { static add(x, y) { return x + y; } } let result = MathUtils.add(5, 3); // Result: 8

Object-Oriented Programming in JavaScript allows developers to model real-world entities as objects, providing a way to structure and organize code. Constructors, prototypes, and inheritance are fundamental concepts for achieving object-oriented designs in JavaScript. ES6 classes introduced a more concise and expressive syntax for creating and extending classes, making object-oriented programming in JavaScript more approachable and modern.

- **Design Patterns in JavaScript**

Singleton Pattern:

1. **Definition:**

- The Singleton Pattern ensures a class has only one instance and provides a global point of access to that instance.

const Singleton = (function () { let instance; function createInstance() { // Private constructor function SingletonInstance() { // Private members this.property = "Singleton Instance"; } return new SingletonInstance(); } return { getInstance: function () { if (!instance) { instance = createInstance(); } return instance; }, }; })(); let singleton1 = Singleton.getInstance(); let singleton2 = Singleton.getInstance(); console.log(singleton1 === singleton2); // Output: true (same instance)

Module Pattern:

1. **Definition:**

- The Module Pattern encapsulates private and public members, providing a way to structure and organize code.

const Module = (function () { // Private members let privateVariable = "I'm private"; function privateFunction() { console.log("This is a private function"); } // Public interface return { publicVariable: "I'm public", publicFunction: function () {

```
console.log("This is a public function"); }, }; })(); console.log(Module.publicVariable); Module.publicFunction();
```

Observer Pattern:

1. **Definition:**

- The Observer Pattern defines a one-to-many dependency between objects so that when one object changes state, all its dependents are notified and updated automatically.

```
class Subject { constructor() { this.observers = []; } addObserver(observer) { this.observers.push(observer); } removeObserver(observer) { this.observers = this.observers.filter((obs) => obs !== observer); } notifyObservers() { this.observers.forEach((observer) => { observer.update(); }); } } class Observer { constructor(name) { this.name = name; } update() { console.log(`${this.name} has been notified.`); } } // Usage let subject = new Subject(); let observer1 = new Observer("Observer 1"); let observer2 = new Observer("Observer 2"); subject.addObserver(observer1); subject.addObserver(observer2); subject.notifyObservers();
```

Design patterns are reusable solutions to common problems in software design. The Singleton Pattern ensures a single instance of a class, the Module Pattern encapsulates private and public members, and the Observer Pattern establishes a dependency between objects. Understanding and applying these patterns can enhance code organization, maintainability, and flexibility in JavaScript applications.

- **Introduction to Testing in JavaScript**

Unit Testing Basics:

1. **Definition:**

- Unit testing involves testing individual units or components of a software application in isolation to ensure they function as expected.

2. **Test Case Structure:**

- A test case typically consists of setup, execution of the code being tested, and assertions to check the expected outcomes.

// Example using a testing library (e.g., Jest) test("Adding 1 + 1 equals 2", () => { // Arrange (setup) const result = add(1, 1); // Act (execute) // Assert (check the expected outcome) expect(result).toBe(2); });

Testing Libraries/Frameworks:

1. **Jest:**

- Jest is a popular JavaScript testing framework with a focus on simplicity. It provides a test runner, assertion library, and mocking capabilities.

// Example Jest test test("Adding 1 + 1 equals 2", () => { expect(add(1, 1)).toBe(2); });

2. **Mocha and Chai:**

- Mocha is a flexible testing framework, and Chai is an assertion library. They are often used together for testing in JavaScript.

// Example Mocha and Chai test const assert = require("chai").assert; describe("Math Operations", () => { it("Adding 1 + 1 equals 2", () => { assert.equal(add(1, 1), 2); }); });

3. **Jasmine:**

- Jasmine is a behavior-driven development (BDD) framework for testing JavaScript code. It provides its own assertion library.

// Example Jasmine test describe("Math Operations", () => { it("Adding 1 + 1 equals 2", () => { expect(add(1, 1)).toBe(2); }); });

Writing Testable Code:

1. **Separation of Concerns:**

- Design code with a clear separation of concerns, making it easier to test individual units.

// Non-testable code function fetchData() { // Makes an API call } // Testable code function fetchData(apiClient) { // Uses the provided API client }

2. **Avoiding Global State:**

- Minimize the reliance on global state, as it can introduce unpredictability in tests.

// Non-testable code let counter = 0; function incrementCounter() { counter++; } // Testable code function incrementCounter(currentValue) { return currentValue + 1; }

3. **Dependency Injection:**

- Use dependency injection to inject dependencies into functions or classes, making it easier to replace dependencies with mock objects during testing.

// Non-testable code function fetchData() { const result = externalAPICall(); // Process result } // Testable code function fetchData(apiClient) { const result = apiClient.fetchData(); // Process result }

Testing in JavaScript is crucial for ensuring code reliability and catching bugs early in the development process. Unit testing, when combined with testing libraries/frameworks, provides a structured approach to verifying the correctness of individual units of code. Writing testable code involves considerations such as separation of concerns, avoiding global state, and using dependency injection to enhance the testability of the codebase.

CHAPTER 4
BUILDING REAL-WORLD APPLICATIONS

- **Building a To-Do List Application**

1. **HTML Structure:**

- Define the structure of the to-do list in HTML, including an input field, a list to display tasks, and buttons for adding and removing tasks.

```
<!DOCTYPE html> <html lang="en"> <head> <meta charset="UTF-8"> <meta name="viewport" content="width=device-width, initial-scale=1.0"> <link rel="stylesheet" href="styles.css"> <title>To-Do List App</title> </head> <body> <div class="container"> <h1>To-Do List</h1> <input type="text" id="taskInput" placeholder="Add a new task"> <button id="addTaskBtn">Add Task</button> <ul id="taskList"></ul> </div> <script src="app.js"></script> </body> </html>
```

2. **CSS Styling:**

- Apply basic styling to create an appealing layout for the to-do list.

body { font-family: 'Arial', sans-serif; background-color: #f4f4f4; margin: 0; padding: 0; display: flex; justify-content: center; align-items: center; height: 100vh; } .container { text-align: center; background-color: #fff; padding: 20px; border-radius: 8px; box-shadow: 0 0 10px rgba(0, 0, 0, 0.1); } h1 { color: #333; } input { padding: 10px; margin-right: 10px; border: 1px solid #ddd; border-radius: 4px; } button { padding: 10px; border: none; background-color: #007bff; color: #fff; cursor: pointer; border-radius: 4px; } ul { list-style-type: none; padding: 0; } li { display: flex; align-items: center; justify-content: space-between; border-bottom: 1px solid #ddd; padding: 8px 0; } .deleteBtn { background-color: #dc3545; }

DOM Manipulation with JavaScript:

1. **Adding Tasks Dynamically:**

- Use JavaScript to manipulate the DOM and add tasks to the to-do list.

document.addEventListener('DOMContentLoaded', function () { const taskInput = document.getElementById('taskInput'); const addTaskBtn = document.getElementById('addTaskBtn'); const taskList = document.getElementById('taskList'); addTaskBtn.addEventListener('click', function () { const taskText = taskInput.value.trim(); if (taskText !== '') { addTask(taskText); taskInput.value = ''; } }); function addTask(taskText) { const li = document.createElement('li'); li.innerHTML = `

```
<span>${taskText}</span> <button class="deleteBtn">Delete</button> `; taskList.appendChild(li); } });
```

Adding Functionality and Styling:

1. **Deleting Tasks:**

- Implement the functionality to delete tasks when the delete button is clicked.

```
document.addEventListener('DOMContentLoaded', function () { // ... (previous code) taskList.addEventListener('click', function (event) { if (event.target.classList.contains('deleteBtn')) { const li = event.target.closest('li'); taskList.removeChild(li); } }); });
```

2. **Styling Completed Tasks:**

- Add styling to differentiate completed tasks.

```
document.addEventListener('DOMContentLoaded', function () { // ... (previous code) taskList.addEventListener('click', function (event) { if (event.target.tagName === 'SPAN') { event.target.classList.toggle('completed'); } else if (event.target.classList.contains('deleteBtn')) { const li = event.target.closest('li'); taskList.removeChild(li); } }); });
```

Creating an Interactive Form:

1. **Interactive Form with Validation:**

- Enhance the form by adding validation and preventing empty or whitespace-only tasks.

```
document.addEventListener('DOMContentLoaded', function () { // ... (previous code) addTaskBtn.addEventListener('click', function () { const taskText = taskInput.value.trim(); if (taskText !== '') { addTask(taskText); taskInput.value = ''; } }); function addTask(taskText) { const li = document.createElement('li'); li.innerHTML = ` <span>${taskText}</span> <button class="deleteBtn">Delete</button> `; taskList.appendChild(li); } taskList.addEventListener('click', function (event) { if (event.target.tagName === 'SPAN') { event.target.classList.toggle('completed'); } else if (event.target.classList.contains('deleteBtn')) { const li = event.target.closest('li'); taskList.removeChild(li); } }); });
```

Building a to-do list application involves setting up the HTML and CSS structure, manipulating the DOM with JavaScript to add tasks dynamically, implementing functionality such as deleting tasks and styling completed tasks, and creating an interactive form with validation. This step-by-step approach helps create a functional and visually appealing to-do list.

- **Implementing a Simple Web Game**

Game Logic and Structure:

1. **HTML Structure:**

- Define the basic HTML structure for the game, including the game container, score display, and game board.

```
<!DOCTYPE html> <html lang="en"> <head> <meta charset="UTF-8"> <meta name="viewport" content="width=device-width, initial-scale=1.0"> <link rel="stylesheet" href="styles.css"> <title>Simple Web Game</title> </head> <body> <div class="game-container"> <h1>Simple Web Game</h1> <p>Score: <span id="score">0</span></p> <div class="game-board" id="gameBoard"></div> </div> <script src="app.js"></script> </body> </html>
```

2. **JavaScript Game Logic:**

- Implement the game logic in JavaScript, including initializing the game, generating random elements, and updating the score.

```
document.addEventListener('DOMContentLoaded', function () { const gameBoard = document.getElementById('gameBoard'); const scoreDisplay = document.getElementById('score'); let score = 0; function initializeGame() { score = 0; updateScore(); generateRandomElement(); } function generateRandomElement() { // Logic to generate and append random elements to the game board
```

} function updateScore() { scoreDisplay.textContent = score; } initializeGame(); });

Event Handling for User Interaction:

1. **Event Handling:**

- Implement event handlers for user interactions, such as clicking on game elements.

document.addEventListener('DOMContentLoaded', function () { // ... (previous code) gameBoard.addEventListener('click', function (event) { if (event.target.classList.contains('game-element')) { // Logic to handle user interaction with game elements score++; updateScore(); generateRandomElement(); } }); });

Styling and Animations:

1. **CSS Styling:**

- Apply basic styling to the game elements for a visually appealing design.

body { font-family: 'Arial', sans-serif; background-color: #f4f4f4; margin: 0; padding: 0; display: flex; justify-content: center; align-items: center; height: 100vh; } .game-container { text-align: center; background-color: #fff; padding: 20px; border-radius: 8px; box-shadow: 0 0 10px rgba(0, 0, 0, 0.1); } .game-board { display: flex; flex-wrap: wrap; gap: 10px; margin-top: 20px; } .game-element { width: 50px; height: 50px; background-color: #007bff;

color: #fff; display: flex; justify-content: center; align-items: center; font-size: 16px; cursor: pointer; } #score { font-weight: bold; color: #007bff; }

- Add animations to game elements to create a more engaging user experience.

.game-element { /* ... (previous styles) */ transition: background-color 0.3s ease-in-out; } .game-element:hover { background-color: #0056b3; }

Building a simple web game involves defining the HTML structure, implementing game logic and structure in JavaScript, handling user interactions with event listeners, and styling the game elements for a visually appealing design. Animations can be added to enhance the user experience. This step-by-step approach helps create a functional and engaging web game.

- **Working with APIs**

1. **Fetch API:**

- Use the Fetch API to make asynchronous requests to a remote API.

function fetchData() { fetch('https://api.example.com/data') .then(response => { if (!response.ok) { throw new Error('Network response was not ok'); } return response.json(); }) .then(data => { // Process the data console.log(data); }) .catch(error => {

console.error('There was a problem with the fetch operation:', error); }); } fetchData();

2. **Async/Await:**

- Alternatively, use async/await syntax for a more readable asynchronous code.

async function fetchData() { try { const response = await fetch('https://api.example.com/data'); if (!response.ok) { throw new Error('Network response was not ok'); } const data = await response.json(); // Process the data console.log(data); } catch (error) { console.error('There was a problem with the fetch operation:', error); } } fetchData();

Parsing API Responses:

1. **JSON Parsing:**

- Most APIs return data in JSON format. Parse the JSON response for further use.

function fetchData() { fetch('https://api.example.com/data') .then(response => { if (!response.ok) { throw new Error('Network response was not ok'); } return response.json(); }) .then(data => { // Process the JSON data console.log(data); }) .catch(error => { console.error('There was a problem with the fetch operation:', error); }); } fetchData();

2. **Handling Different Data Formats:**

- Adjust parsing based on the API's response format (e.g., JSON, XML).

```
function fetchData() { fetch('https://api.example.com/data') .then(response => { if (!response.ok) { throw new Error('Network response was not ok'); } // Check the content type const contentType = response.headers.get('content-type'); if (contentType.includes('application/json')) { return response.json(); } else if (contentType.includes('text/xml')) { return response.text(); } else { throw new Error('Unsupported content type'); } }) .then(data => { // Process the data based on its format console.log(data); }) .catch(error => { console.error('There was a problem with the fetch operation:', error); }); } fetchData();
```

Integrating External Data into Your Application:

1. **Rendering Data in HTML:**

- Integrate the external data into your application by rendering it dynamically in HTML.

```
function fetchDataAndRender() { fetch('https://api.example.com/data') .then(response => { if (!response.ok) { throw new Error('Network response was not ok'); } return response.json(); }) .then(data => { // Render the data in the HTML renderData(data); }) .catch(error => { console.error('There was a problem with the fetch operation:', error); }); } function
```

renderData(data) { const container = document.getElementById('dataContainer'); container.innerHTML = ''; data.forEach(item => { const listItem = document.createElement('li'); listItem.textContent = item.name; container.appendChild(listItem); }); } fetchDataAndRender();

2. **Updating Application State:**

- Update the application state with the fetched data for dynamic interactions.

let appState = { data: [], }; function fetchDataAndUpdateState() { fetch('https://api.example.com/data') .then(response => { if (!response.ok) { throw new Error('Network response was not ok'); } return response.json(); }) .then(data => { // Update the application state appState.data = data; // Trigger UI updates or other actions updateUI(); }) .catch(error => { console.error('There was a problem with the fetch operation:', error); }); } function updateUI() { // Update the UI based on the application state console.log('UI updated with new data:', appState.data); } fetchDataAndUpdateState();

Working with APIs involves making HTTP requests with JavaScript, parsing the API responses, and integrating external data into your application. Use the Fetch API for making requests, parse JSON responses, and adapt to different data formats if needed.

Integrating external data includes rendering it in HTML and updating the application state for dynamic interactions.

- **Introduction to Node.js**

1. **Node.js Installation:**

- Download and install Node.js from the official website (https://nodejs.org/).

- Verify the installation by running the following commands in the terminal:

```
node -v npm -v
```

2. **npm Initialization:**

- Create a **package.json** file for managing dependencies and project configuration.

```
npm init -y
```

3. **Installing Express:**

- Install Express.js, a popular web framework for Node.js.

```
npm install express
```

Writing a Simple Server:

1. **Basic Server Script:**

- Create a simple Node.js script to set up a server using the **http** module.

```
const http = require('http'); const server = http.createServer((req, res) => { res.writeHead(200, { 'Content-Type': 'text/plain' }); res.end('Hello, Node.js!'); }); const PORT = 3000; server.listen(PORT, () => { console.log(`Server running on http://localhost:${PORT}`); });
```

2. **Running the Server:**

- Run the server script using the following command:

```
node server.js
```

3. **Accessing the Server:**

- Open a web browser and navigate to **http://localhost:3000**. You should see the message "Hello, Node.js!"

Building a Basic Express.js Application:

1. **Express.js Setup:**

- Create an Express.js application by setting up a basic server script.

```
const express = require('express'); const app = express(); const PORT = 3000; app.get('/', (req, res) => { res.send('Hello, Express!'); }); app.listen(PORT, () => { console.log(`Express app listening on http://localhost:${PORT}`); });
```

2. **Middleware and Routing:**

- Add middleware and define routes in the Express application.

const express = require('express'); const app = express(); const PORT = 3000; // Middleware for logging requests app.use((req, res, next) => { console.log(`[${new Date().toLocaleString()}] ${req.method} ${req.url}`); next(); }); // Route for the home page app.get('/', (req, res) => { res.send('Hello, Express!'); }); // Route for another page app.get('/about', (req, res) => { res.send('About Us'); }); app.listen(PORT, () => { console.log(`Express app listening on http://localhost:${PORT}`); });

3. **Static File Serving:**

- Use Express to serve static files, such as HTML, CSS, and images.

const express = require('express'); const app = express(); const PORT = 3000; // Serve static files from the "public" directory app.use(express.static('public')); // Route for the home page app.get('/', (req, res) => { res.send('Hello, Express!'); }); app.listen(PORT, () => { console.log(`Express app listening on http://localhost:${PORT}`); });

Node.js provides a runtime environment for server-side JavaScript, allowing the development of scalable and efficient web applications. Setting up a Node.js environment involves installing Node.js and npm, initializing a **package.json** file, and installing necessary dependencies. Writing a simple server using the **http** module and building a basic Express.js application demonstrate the fundamentals of server-side development with Node.js. Express.js simplifies the creation of web applications by providing a robust framework for handling routes, middleware, and static file serving.

CHAPTER 5

BEST PRACTICES AND OPTIMIZATION

- **Code Organization and Maintainability**

1. **Folder Structure:**

- Organize your project into meaningful folders, separating concerns like routes, controllers, models, and static assets.

/project ├── /controllers ├── /models ├── /routes ├── /public ├── app.js ├── package.json

2. **Modularization:**

- Break down your code into reusable and modular components. Use modules for specific functionalities.

// controllers/userController.js const getUser = (req, res) => { // Logic to get user data }; module.exports = { getUser, };

// routes/userRoutes.js const express = require('express'); const userController = require('../controllers/userController'); const router = express.Router(); router.get('/user', userController.getUser); module.exports = router;

// app.js const express = require('express'); const userRoutes = require('./routes/userRoutes'); const app = express(); app.use('/api', userRoutes); const PORT = 3000; app.listen(PORT, () => { console.log(`Server running on http://localhost:${PORT}`); });

3. **Middleware Usage:**

- Utilize middleware for common functionalities such as logging, error handling, and authentication.

// middleware/logger.js const logger = (req, res, next) => { console.log(`[${new Date().toLocaleString()}] ${req.method} ${req.url}`); next(); }; module.exports = logger;

// app.js const express = require('express'); const logger = require('./middleware/logger'); const app = express(); app.use(logger); // ... other middleware and routes

4. **Error Handling:**

- Implement a centralized error-handling mechanism to enhance code maintainability.

// middleware/errorHandler.js const errorHandler = (err, req, res, next) => { console.error(err.stack); res.status(500).send('Internal Server Error'); }; module.exports = errorHandler;

// app.js const express = require('express'); const errorHandler = require('./middleware/errorHandler'); const app = express(); // ... other middleware and routes app.use(errorHandler);

Performance Optimization:

1. **Caching:**

- Implement caching for frequently accessed data to reduce response time.

```
const cache = {}; const getUser = (req, res) => { const userId = req.params.id; if (cache[userId]) { res.json(cache[userId]); } else { // Logic to fetch user data const userData = /* ... */; cache[userId] = userData; res.json(userData); } };
```

2. **Compression:**

- Use compression middleware to reduce the size of responses.

```
const express = require('express'); const compression = require('compression'); const app = express(); app.use(compression());
```

3. **Database Indexing:**

- Optimize database queries by adding indexes to frequently queried fields.

```
// MongoDB index example db.collection('users').createIndex({ username: 1 });
```

4. **Load Balancing:**

- Distribute incoming traffic across multiple servers using load balancing to improve performance and reliability.

```
// Example with the 'express-http-proxy' middleware const express = require('express'); const proxy = require('express-http-proxy'); const app = express(); app.use('/api', proxy('http://server1:3000')); app.use('/api', proxy('http://server2:3000'));
```

5. **Client-Side Optimizations:**

- Optimize client-side assets (CSS, JavaScript, images) and use techniques like lazy loading to improve page load times.

```
<!-- Example for lazy-loading images --> <img src="placeholder.jpg" data-src="image.jpg" loading="lazy" alt="Lazy-loaded Image">
```

Code organization and maintainability are crucial for long-term development. Utilize a clear folder structure, modularize code, use middleware effectively, and implement error handling for a maintainable codebase. For performance optimization, consider caching, compression, database indexing, load balancing, and client-side optimizations to enhance the overall efficiency of your application.

- **Security Best Practices**

1. **Input Validation:**

- Always validate and sanitize user inputs to prevent injection attacks.

// Example with Express.js middleware const express = require('express'); const app = express(); app.use(express.json()); app.post('/login', (req, res) => { const { username, password } = req.body; // Validate inputs to prevent SQL injection if (!username || !password) { return res.status(400).json({ error: 'Invalid input' }); } // Process login logic // ... });

2. **Authentication and Authorization:**

- Use secure authentication mechanisms like JWT (JSON Web Tokens) and implement proper authorization checks.

const jwt = require('jsonwebtoken'); // Example of generating and verifying JWT const token = jwt.sign({ user: 'john.doe' }, 'secretKey', { expiresIn: '1h' }); const decoded = jwt.verify(token, 'secretKey');

3. **HTTPS Usage:**

- Always use HTTPS to encrypt data transmitted between the client and the server.

const https = require('https'); const fs = require('fs'); const options = { key: fs.readFileSync('server-key.pem'), cert:

```
fs.readFileSync('server-cert.pem'), }; https.createServer(options, (req, res) => { // Handle HTTPS requests }).listen(3000);
```

4. **Security Headers:**

- Set security headers to mitigate common web vulnerabilities.

```
const helmet = require('helmet'); const app = express(); app.use(helmet());
```

5. **Dependency Scanning:**

- Regularly scan dependencies for known vulnerabilities using tools like npm audit.

```
npm audit
```

Accessibility in JavaScript:

1. **Semantic HTML:**

- Use semantic HTML elements to provide a meaningful structure to your content.

```
<header> <h1>Page Title</h1> </header> <nav> <ul> <li><a href="/">Home</a></li> <li><a href="/about">About</a></li> <li><a href="/contact">Contact</a></li> </ul> </nav> <main> <!-
```

```
- Main content --> </main> <footer> <!-- Footer content -->
</footer>
```

2. **Keyboard Navigation:**

- Ensure that all interactive elements are accessible via keyboard navigation.

```
<button onclick="myFunction()" onkeydown="if(event.key === 'Enter') myFunction()">Click me</button>
```

3. **Accessible Forms:**

- Include proper labels, use ARIA roles, and ensure forms are easily navigable.

```
<label for="username">Username:</label> <input type="text" id="username" name="username" required>
```

4. **Contrast and Text Size:**

- Maintain sufficient color contrast and provide options for users to adjust text size.

```
body { color: #333; background-color: #fff; font-size: 16px; }
```

5. **Aria Attributes:**

- Use ARIA (Accessible Rich Internet Applications) attributes to enhance accessibility for dynamic content.

```
<div role="alert" aria-live="assertive">Error message!</div>
```

6. **Screen Reader Testing:**

- Test your application with screen readers to ensure compatibility and a positive user experience.

<!-- Example of hiding an element visually but making it accessible to screen readers --> <span class="visually-hidden">This text is hidden but accessible</span>

JavaScript plays a crucial role in building secure and accessible web applications. Follow security best practices, such as input validation, secure authentication, HTTPS usage, and implementing security headers. For accessibility, focus on using semantic HTML, providing keyboard navigation, creating accessible forms, maintaining proper contrast and text size, utilizing ARIA attributes, and conducting thorough screen reader testing.

- **Continuous Learning and Resources**

Embracing Continuous Learning:

1. **Stay Updated with Documentation:**

- Regularly review the official documentation of the technologies you are working with. Updates and new features are often documented, providing valuable insights. Familiarize yourself with release notes to understand the latest changes.

2. **Follow Blogs and Newsletters:**

- Subscribe to blogs, newsletters, and forums related to web development. Authors often share their experiences, best practices, and updates on emerging technologies. Consider platforms like Medium, where many developers contribute insightful articles.

3. **Participate in Online Communities:**

- Join online communities such as Stack Overflow, Reddit (e.g., r/webdev), or specialized forums. Engage in discussions, ask questions, and learn from the experiences of others. Actively participating in community-driven platforms can provide diverse perspectives.

4. **Attend Webinars and Conferences:**

- Attend webinars, virtual meetups, and online conferences. These events provide opportunities to learn from experts, discover new tools, and connect with the broader developer community. Platforms like Zoom and YouTube often host these events.

5. **Online Courses and Platforms:**

- Enroll in online courses on platforms like Udemy, Coursera, or LinkedIn Learning. Many courses cover a wide range of topics, from programming languages to advanced frameworks.

Consider both free and paid courses based on your learning preferences.

6. **Contribute to Open Source:**

- Contribute to open-source projects on platforms like GitHub. Engaging in collaborative development not only enhances your coding skills but also exposes you to diverse coding styles and project structures.

7. **Pair Programming:**

- Engage in pair programming sessions with peers or mentors. Collaborative coding not only improves your problem-solving skills but also exposes you to different approaches and coding techniques.

8. **Keep a Learning Journal:**

- Maintain a learning journal to document your progress, challenges faced, and solutions discovered. Reflecting on your learning journey helps reinforce concepts and identify areas for improvement.

Recommended Resources:

1. **Web Development Learning Platforms:**

- MDN Web Docs: Comprehensive documentation and guides on web technologies. Explore not only the basics but also advanced topics like web APIs.

- W3Schools: Tutorials and references for web development technologies. The platform offers interactive coding exercises for hands-on practice.
- freeCodeCamp: Free interactive coding challenges and projects. The platform emphasizes project-based learning.

2. **Blogs and Newsletters:**

- Smashing Magazine: Articles on web design and development. Dive into their extensive archives for in-depth reads on various topics.
- CSS-Tricks: Tips, tricks, and guides for front-end development. Explore their "Almanac" section for detailed CSS guides.
- Dev.to: A community of developers sharing knowledge and experiences. Follow specific tags or topics of interest.

3. **Online Courses:**

- Coursera: Offers courses from universities and organizations around the world. Check for specializations and certificates.

- Udemy: Provides a wide range of courses on various topics, often at affordable prices. Look for highly rated courses with practical projects.
- LinkedIn Learning: Video tutorials on web development, design, and business skills. Explore learning paths for a structured approach.

4. **Books:**

- "Eloquent JavaScript" by Marijn Haverbeke: A book for learning JavaScript. The online version is interactive, allowing you to code within the book.
- "You Don't Know JS" by Kyle Simpson: A series of books delving into the intricacies of JavaScript. Ideal for those seeking a deeper understanding.
- "Clean Code" by Robert C. Martin: Focuses on writing clean, maintainable code. Considered a classic in software development literature.

5. **Podcasts:**

- Syntax: A podcast about web development with Wes Bos and Scott Tolinski. Episodes cover both beginner-friendly and advanced topics.

- ShopTalk Show: A podcast about front-end web design, development, and UX. The hosts discuss current trends and challenges.

6. **Version Control:**

- Git Documentation: Official documentation for Git. Delve into advanced topics like rebasing and branching.

- GitHub Learning Lab: Interactive courses on using Git and GitHub. Perfect for hands-on learning.

7. **Advanced Topics:**

- Mozilla Developer Network (MDN) - JavaScript Guide: In-depth guide to JavaScript. Explore advanced JavaScript concepts.

- Node.js Documentation: Documentation for Node.js and its packages. Learn about building scalable server-side applications.

8. **Security and Best Practices:**

- OWASP: Open Web Application Security Project provides resources on web application security. Stay updated on security best practices.

- Web.dev: Google's resource for modern web development best practices. Includes tools for assessing website performance and accessibility.

Continuous learning in web development involves a holistic approach, incorporating diverse resources and learning styles. Tailor your learning journey to your goals, and remember that curiosity is a developer's best companion. Build projects, contribute to the community, and stay inspired by the ever-evolving world of web development.

CONCLUSION

In the ever-evolving landscape of web development, the journey of continuous learning is not just a pathway but a dynamic adventure. Embracing this journey requires a multifaceted approach, integrating various resources and learning styles. The principles of staying updated, engaging with communities, and participating in collaborative endeavors form the bedrock of a successful learning expedition.

Continuous Learning Dynamics: Staying updated with official documentation ensures that you are well-versed in the latest features, optimizations, and best practices of the technologies you engage with. Subscribing to blogs, newsletters, and participating in online communities fosters a sense of connection and shared knowledge within the vast web development ecosystem. Virtual events, webinars, and conferences become invaluable opportunities to glean insights from experts and discover emerging trends.

Interactive Learning Spaces: Online platforms, with their plethora of courses and tutorials, serve as interactive learning spaces. From foundational knowledge to advanced concepts, platforms like Coursera, Udemy, and LinkedIn Learning offer a diverse range of courses to cater to various learning preferences. Contribute to open-source projects on platforms like GitHub to immerse yourself in real-world coding scenarios, honing both technical skills and collaborative practices.

Resourceful Recommendations: A rich repository of resources, ranging from authoritative documentation to immersive podcasts, ensures a well-rounded learning experience. Books such as "Eloquent JavaScript" and "Clean Code" offer deep dives into programming concepts and best practices. Podcasts like "Syntax" and "ShopTalk Show" bring the community's voices and experiences to your ears, fostering a sense of camaraderie.

Specialized Areas of Focus: Web development encompasses a vast array of topics, from fundamental languages like HTML, CSS, and JavaScript to specialized areas such as security, performance optimization, and accessibility. Delving into advanced topics like those covered by the OWASP project and Google's Web.dev ensures a comprehensive understanding of security practices and modern web development standards.

The Art of Continuous Reflection: Maintaining a learning journal becomes an art of continuous reflection, allowing you to track your progress, document challenges, and celebrate victories. Pair programming sessions and engaging with mentors provide dynamic learning experiences, fostering an environment of shared knowledge and growth.

In conclusion, continuous learning in web development is not just a pursuit; it's a mindset. It's about staying curious, adapting to change, and finding joy in the process. As the web continues to evolve, so does the journey of a web developer. Through diverse resources, collaboration, and an insatiable appetite for knowledge, you not only navigate the challenges but also shape the future of web development. So, embrace the journey, immerse yourself in the dynamic ecosystem, and let the pursuit of knowledge be the compass guiding you toward mastery and innovation. Happy coding!

www.ingramcontent.com/pod-product-compliance
Lightning Source LLC
LaVergne TN
LVHW022006200926
848481LV00007B/2257
9798215770931